*In loving memory of a wonderful
husband and father, David Borthwick*

For Jane and Louisa

Published by C.R. Gibson®
C. R. Gibson® is a registered trademark of Thomas Nelson, Inc., Nashville, Tennessee 37214
Design by Anderson Thomas Design, Nashville, Tennessee.
Cover Photography © 1999 Russ Harrington

Printed in Mexico

ISBN 0-7667-6661-6
GB512R

From

Mother

with

Love

For My

Daughter

by Evelyn Borthwick

From the moment I knew for sure

That you were on the way

My heart stood still, the words were lost,

I knew not what to say.

Was I really ready?

However would I know?

I guess it didn't matter;

I just knew I'd love you so.

And as I felt you growing,

This miracle of mine,

My eyes grew large with wonder

Like stars they seemed to shine.

Dear Lord, let me be worthy

To receive this treasured soul,

This tiny little person

That one day will make me whole.

As I glance into my mirror
I can't believe my eyes!
Is that really me in there?
I can't believe my size!
And with my hands I feel you,
As you move inside of me,
And with my eyes I watch you,
Seems you're all that I can see.
And even now I love you,
And long to hold you tight.
Even though I'm nervous,
Will I make it through the night?
So hurry little treasure
As I can barely wait.
The time is NOW – I know it!
Please hurry – don't be late!

The time went by so quickly,
And suddenly it's here,
The moment that I longed for;
I no longer seem to fear.
You'll soon be here beside me
In your special little place.
And I'll be so excited,
When I see your tiny face.
Welcome, darling daughter
My greatest dream come true.
My heart is yours forever
It will always be for you.
And in this world of changes
I'll do my very best
To teach you all the good things
And protect you from the rest.

Here we are together
The way that it should be.
I watch you sleep and wonder
Do you really look like me?
Your little face, your tiny hands
And tiny little toes.
Lying now, so peacefully,
My pride and pleasure shows.
I want so much to hold you,
To keep you in my arms,
To always be there for you,
And succumb to all your charms.
To make you feel so safe,
So happy and secure,
And have you understand that
No one else could love you more.

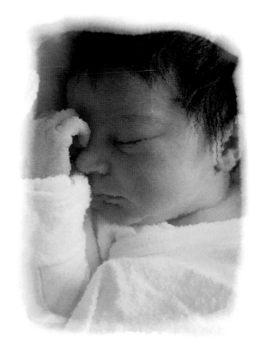

As I watch you growing
Right here before my eyes,
You're bright and so adorable
And it's no surprise.
I see you stretch and reach,
And let it be known
You want me there beside you.
You don't like it on your own.
I watch you with such pleasure,
As you smile and you play.
No wonder I adore you,
You always make my day.
Sweet baby – how I love you –
I know I always will,
With you right here beside me,
My life is now fulfilled.

The day I really worried,
Was the day that you were sick.
With watery eyes and runny nose –
I called the doctor quick.
And had him reassure me
That you would be all right,
Even though he laughed and said,
That I'd not sleep that night.
Yes teething sure was painful,
And wouldn't let you sleep.
I'd walk with you in my arms,
Round the room I'd creep.
So slowly, as I soothed you,
The pain drifted away.
And in my arms, so warm and snug,
Was where you'd want to stay.

You're up and off and crawling
It's fun to watch you go.
Discovering all those new things,
It's just as if you know,
That this is part of growing
And learning while you play,
Whilst getting rid of obstacles
That dare get in your way!
You're really quite determined,
I can see it in your face.
You grab and pull and push things
And knock them from their place.
And when you get frustrated,
You cry and often pout,
And look at me as if to say,
"Please Mommy, help me out!"

Baby, it's your first Christmas
There are so many sights,
Soft white snow and mistletoe,
And all the pretty lights.
The tree with all the presents
Wrapped so bright and gay,
Entices you to its corner
Where you can sit and play.
Oh, Baby, you're so happy,
With all these things you see.
I join you in your corner
And you climb onto my knee.
And as we laugh together;
There's so much joy I feel
I pull you a little closer;
While a little kiss I steal.

It's your first birthday, Sweetheart.
The year went by so fast!
No more a tiny baby;
But a little girl at last.
A little girl in dresses,
With buttons and with bows.
A little girl so pretty,
From her head down to her toes,
With your cake and candle
And pictures that we'll treasure,
It's fun to see you laughing
You give me so much pleasure.
You'll always be my Princess,
My little star so bright.
With you life is so wonderful,
You make the dark days bright.

Your second year is special
You learn a little more.
You knew that one and one make two,
And two and two make four.
You mimic all my actions,
Watch everything I do.
Trying, oh so patiently,
Soon you can do it, too.
It's a year of much frustration,
A year of time well spent.
A year that just flew right on by,
I wonder where it went?
A year of independence,
And, no matter if I'd groan,
You were quite determined
To do it on your own.

Time goes by so quickly,
It's amazing how you grow,
And how you talk and chatter;
To tell me all you know.
You really do amaze me,
You're learning every day.
I will just encourage you,
And not get in your way.
The questions that you ask me —
The things you say and do!
"Is the moon really made of cheese?"
"Did a lady live in a shoe?"
Yes, darling keep on asking,
'Cause that's the way you learn.
And I will do my very best
To teach you in return.

With great anticipation,
And very little sleep,
I'm so very nervous,
As I have a little weep.
I feel a little stupid.
I feel like such a fool!
But try to understand because
It's your first day of school!
"Oh, please let her enjoy it,"
I say my silent prayer.
"And let her day be special,
Without me being there.
Please let this day be pleasant,
'Cause I'm feeling so much pain,
And let this day go quickly
So I'll have her home again."

At school your days seem happy
I'm very pleased to say,
And you don't seem to mind it
As you wave me on your way.
But still, I really miss you,
And I will have to try
To understand my sadness,
And resolve my reasons why.
I guess because you're growing,
And time just won't stand still,
And I'm the one who needs you,
I guess I always will.
So try to understand me,
As silly as it seems
You'll always be my baby girl,
If only in my dreams.

In school your friends were many
You'd bring them home to play.
And often you would ask me,
"Oh, please Mommy, may they stay?"
And I had no objections
Your friends were always good,
They loved to play here with you
As often as they could.
You'd giggle in your bedroom,
Be awake for half the night,
And in the morning daybreak
You'd awaken with the light.
I love to see you have fun,
Childhood goes so fast
And things that made you happy,
Well…I'd want to make them last.

With all those childhood ailments
Like chicken pox and mumps,
It's not surprising that at times
You were down and in the dumps.
So I would tuck you in your bed
And sit with you a while,
I'd tell you silly stories
Just to make you smile!
I'd buy you little presents,
And make you lots of treats
And sort out special candies
And your favourite kinds of sweets.
It helped to make you better;
And not feel quite so sad.
And realize, those days in bed
Didn't have to be so bad.

On weekends we would laugh
As stories we'd unfold
Of funny ghosts and goblins,
Too silly to behold.
And later I would go
To the kitchen to make tea.
We'd bring it to the porch
Just for you and me.
We'd dress at our leisure,
Have breakfast and then…
Maybe tell stories all over again?

The times that we went shopping,
I guess I loved them best.
Yes, even when you proved to be,
At times a little pest!
We'd look in all the windows,
At clothes, and books and toys,
And now and then I'd see you smile
So shyly at the boys.
When the day was over;
And we'd walked right off our feet,
We'd go to some nice restaurant
And have a bite to eat.
Then home with all our packages,
We'd toss them in a heap,
And curl up on the sofa
To have a little sleep.

I remember the first time
You simply said, "No!"
I couldn't believe it,
You upset me so.

You needed to make it
Perfectly clear;
That this was your right,
I had nothing to fear.

And you were a person
With a mind of your own.
And I was a grown-up,
I should have known.

For this was my teaching,
How could it be wrong?
It's all part of growing,
And making you strong.

From grade school to high school,
The years just flew by.
I'd watch you in wonder;
Then sit back and sigh.
To share with each other
Our days — good and bad,

To share all our news,
Be it happy or sad.
To know that you love me,
The way I love you.
These things are so precious,
I can't believe how time flew.

You'd watch me do my make up
And ask if you just might,
Experiment a little,
And learn to do it right.
I would sit and watch you
And help you if you asked.
Oh how the time was flying –
Growing up so fast.
The results were quite amazing
And you could see it, too.
No longer just a little girl,
Was something we both knew.
And there was a tiny aching,
And I could feel the pain
And long to hold you in my arms,
My little girl again.

Decisions, decisions —
Which dress will you wear?
And what will you do,
When it comes to your hair?
"This boy is so special,"
You said with a sigh,
"It's got to be perfect,
Or else I'll just die!"
You looked simply lovely,
So pretty, so sweet.
With heart beating wildly —
This young man to meet,
Your eyes danced and sparkled
As you left on your date.
And softly I whispered,
"Please dear — don't be late!"

The time you went off,
On that special date —
You whispered to me
That you might be quite late.
I tried not to worry,
But try as I might,
I still had this fear
I'd wait up all night.

And wonder how would I deal
With this feeling I had?
How much was my business?
Should I be sad?
I chose to trust you,
It was your choice to make,
I know you had learned
The right path to take.

"*It's over, it's finished – I hate him*
We're through."
So how could I like him?
Your pain hurts me, too!
That first love's the hardest,
With ups and with downs.
With smiles and with laughter;
With tears and with frowns.
But sweetheart, hang in there,
That heartache will go.
It happens to all of us
Believe me – I know.
And one day the right man
Will enter your life.
And he'll be so happy
To make you his wife.

There are times that I remember
When angry words were spoken,
Especially if you lied to me,
And promises were broken.
Who said that life was easy,
And things would go your way?
Well now you know it isn't,
And sometimes you have to pay.
It hurts me to upset you,
I hate to see you cry.
But sometimes these things happen,
No matter how we try.
I hate those confrontations.
I hate it when we fight,
Yet when it's over, we know
It will turn out all right.

With mutual respect,
We still have our own views.
And you can believe in
Whatever you choose.
It's fun to debate you,
And have a small fight.
I see you so strong now,
Stand up for what's right.
You know I admire you,
You walk a straight line.
Your mind is so firm,
It's as stubborn as mine!
You'll go far; I know it,
I feel so much pride
A feeling of love,
That this mom just can't hide.

A young woman now,
With beauty and grace.
With warmth and compassion
That shows on your face;
You're caring and loving,
I knew you would be.
It's the way that I taught you,
Will you be like me?
Your peers and your friends
Are important, it's true,
You make sure they know it
They matter to you.
I'm proud of your standards
Your ethics so fine,
But most of all, sweetheart,
I'm proud that you're mine.

It's hard when deciding
The right route to take,
With future decisions,
There's so much at stake.
If you feel that you're right,
In whatever you choose,
Stand by your decision,
You'll have nothing to lose.

To earn well and be happy,
Is the major goal.
To be able to do this
And not sell your soul.
For haven't I taught you
That life can be sweet,
If ambitions and dreams
Should just happen to meet.

Sometimes I sit and daydream,
Of all the things we've done.
The years have passed so quickly,
And still we have such fun.
You really understand me,
I love the time we spend
Together with each other;
You are my dearest friend.
You share with me your secrets,
Your passions and your fears.
I share with you my laughter;
My sadness and my tears.
I can't imagine ever;
My life without you there,
And that's my way of telling you,
How much I really care.

To be a mom is wonderful,
Believe me, this is true.
Especially to be the mom
Of a daughter just like you.
A daughter who helped make me
What I am today,
A daughter very special,
In each and every way.
And knowing I helped mold you
Makes me very proud.
Because believe me, Sweetheart –
You stand out among the crowd.
Don't change a thing about you
You're perfect as you are.
And with your charm and character
I know that you'll go far.

By now I hope you know,
I love you...
And know how much I care.
Whenever you may need me,
Just call, and I'll be there.
And if sometime I can't be,
And you're a little blue
Just read these honest words
And I'll be close to you.
My wish is very simple –
I would like to be
The kind of mom to you,
As my mom was to me.
And one day, I pray that you
Will have a lovely daughter; too.
I hope that she will be,
A daughter just like you.